GOD HEARS HER
planner

This planner belongs to:

_____

If found, please contact me:

_____

Cover design by Patti Brinks
Cover illustration by McKenna Bice

ISBN: 978-1-64070-349-0

Printed in China
24 25 26 27 28 29 / 6 5 4 3 2 1

MONTH:

MONDAY

TUESDAY

WEDNESDAY

THURSDAY

FRIDAY

SATURDAY

SUNDAY

Because he turned his ear to me, I will call on him as long as I live. —PSALM 116:2 NIV

MONDAY

TUESDAY

WEDNESDAY

THURSDAY

FRIDAY

SATURDAY

SUNDAY

May he give us the desire to do his will in everything. —1 KINGS 8:58 NLT

MONTH:

MONDAY

TUESDAY

WEDNESDAY

THURSDAY

FRIDAY

SATURDAY

SUNDAY

MONTH:

MONDAY

TUESDAY

WEDNESDAY

THURSDAY

FRIDAY

SATURDAY

SUNDAY

We wait in hope for the Lord; he is our help and our shield. —PSALM 33:20 NIV

MONTH:

MONDAY

TUESDAY

WEDNESDAY

THURSDAY

FRIDAY

SATURDAY

SUNDAY

The LORD is a mighty tower where his people can run for safety. —PROVERBS 18:10 CEV

MONTH:

MONDAY

TUESDAY

WEDNESDAY

THURSDAY

FRIDAY

SATURDAY

SUNDAY

The plan of the LORD stands forever, the plans of His heart from generation to generation.

—PSALM 33:11 NASB

MONTH:

MONDAY

TUESDAY

WEDNESDAY

THURSDAY

FRIDAY

SATURDAY

SUNDAY

For this is what the Sovereign LORD says: I myself will search for my sheep and look after them.

—EZEKIEL 34:11 NIV

The Word became flesh and
made his dwelling among us.
We have seen his glory, the
glory of the one and only Son,
who came from the Father,
full of grace and truth.

—JOHN 1:14 NIV

MONTH:

MONDAY

TUESDAY

WEDNESDAY

THURSDAY

FRIDAY

SATURDAY

SUNDAY

Taste and see that the LORD is good; blessed is the one who takes refuge in him. —PSALM 34:8 NIV

MONDAY

TUESDAY

WEDNESDAY

THURSDAY

FRIDAY

SATURDAY

SUNDAY

Everything else is worthless when compared with the infinite value of knowing Christ Jesus my Lord.

—PHILIPPIANS 3:8 NLT

MONTH:

MONDAY

TUESDAY

WEDNESDAY

THURSDAY

FRIDAY

SATURDAY

SUNDAY

He is the living God, and steadfast forever. —DANIEL 6:26 NKJV

MONTH:

MONDAY

TUESDAY

WEDNESDAY

THURSDAY

FRIDAY

SATURDAY

SUNDAY

Clothe yourselves with the Lord Jesus Christ. —ROMANS 13:14 NIV

MONDAY

TUESDAY

WEDNESDAY

THURSDAY

FRIDAY

SATURDAY

SUNDAY

MONTH:

MONDAY

TUESDAY

WEDNESDAY

THURSDAY

FRIDAY

SATURDAY

SUNDAY

MONDAY

TUESDAY

WEDNESDAY

THURSDAY

FRIDAY

SATURDAY

SUNDAY

Love the Lord your God with all your heart and with all your soul
and with all your mind and with all your strength. —MARK 12:30 NIV

MONDAY

TUESDAY

WEDNESDAY

THURSDAY

FRIDAY

SATURDAY

SUNDAY

Seek his will in all you do, and he will show you which path to take. —PROVERBS 3:6 NLT

MONTH:

MONDAY

TUESDAY

WEDNESDAY

THURSDAY

FRIDAY

SATURDAY

SUNDAY

Thank God! He gives us victory over sin and death through our Lord Jesus Christ.

—1 CORINTHIANS 15:57 NLT

MONDAY

TUESDAY

WEDNESDAY

THURSDAY

FRIDAY

SATURDAY

SUNDAY

MONDAY

TUESDAY

WEDNESDAY

THURSDAY

FRIDAY

SATURDAY

SUNDAY

The steadfast love of the LORD never ceases; his mercies never come to an end.

—LAMENTATIONS 3:22 ESV

MONDAY

TUESDAY

WEDNESDAY

THURSDAY

FRIDAY

SATURDAY

SUNDAY

"I will never leave you or abandon you." —HEBREWS 13:5 CSB

MONTH:

MONDAY

TUESDAY

WEDNESDAY

THURSDAY

FRIDAY

SATURDAY

SUNDAY

Guard your heart above all else, for it determines the course of your life. —PROVERBS 4:23 NLT

MONDAY

TUESDAY

WEDNESDAY

THURSDAY

FRIDAY

SATURDAY

SUNDAY

God proves his own love for us in that while we were still sinners,
Christ died for us. —ROMANS 5:8 CSB

MONTH:

MONDAY

TUESDAY

WEDNESDAY

THURSDAY

FRIDAY

SATURDAY

SUNDAY

The LORD will give strength to His people; the LORD will bless His people with peace.

—PSALM 29:11 NASB

I pray that you, being rooted
and established in love,
may have power, together
with all the Lord's holy
people, to grasp how wide
and long and high and
deep is the love of Christ.

—EPHESIANS 3:17–18 NIV

MONTH:

MONDAY

TUESDAY

WEDNESDAY

THURSDAY

FRIDAY

SATURDAY

SUNDAY

He lets me lie down in green pastures; He leads me beside quiet waters. He restores my soul.

—PSALM 23:2–3 NASB

MONTH:

MONDAY

TUESDAY

WEDNESDAY

THURSDAY

FRIDAY

SATURDAY

SUNDAY

I have learned in whatever situation I am to be content. —PHILIPPIANS 4:11 ESV

MONDAY

TUESDAY

WEDNESDAY

THURSDAY

FRIDAY

SATURDAY

SUNDAY

You know everything I do in more detail than even I know. —PSALM 139:3 VOICE

MONDAY

TUESDAY

WEDNESDAY

THURSDAY

FRIDAY

SATURDAY

SUNDAY

Always be humble and gentle. Patiently put up with each other and love each other.

—EPHESIANS 4:2 CEV

MONDAY

TUESDAY

WEDNESDAY

THURSDAY

FRIDAY

SATURDAY

SUNDAY

God is the one who began this good work in you, and . . . he won't stop
before it is complete on the day that Christ Jesus returns. —PHILIPPIANS 1:6 CEV

MONTH:

MONDAY

TUESDAY

WEDNESDAY

THURSDAY

FRIDAY

SATURDAY

SUNDAY

Nothing you do for the Lord is ever useless. —1 CORINTHIANS 15:58 NLT

MONTH:

MONDAY

TUESDAY

WEDNESDAY

THURSDAY

FRIDAY

SATURDAY

SUNDAY

We love because he first loved us. —1 JOHN 4:19 NIV

MONDAY

TUESDAY

WEDNESDAY

THURSDAY

FRIDAY

SATURDAY

SUNDAY

"Call to Me, and I will answer you." —JEREMIAH 33:3 NKJV

MONTH:

MONDAY

TUESDAY

WEDNESDAY

THURSDAY

FRIDAY

SATURDAY

SUNDAY

The unfading beauty of a gentle and quiet spirit . . . is of great worth in God's sight. —1 PETER 3:4 NIV

MONDAY

TUESDAY

WEDNESDAY

THURSDAY

FRIDAY

SATURDAY

SUNDAY

"If you are tired from carrying heavy burdens,
come to me and I will give you rest." —MATTHEW 11:28 CEV

MONTH:

MONDAY

TUESDAY

WEDNESDAY

THURSDAY

FRIDAY

SATURDAY

SUNDAY

The LORD your God is with you, the Mighty Warrior who saves. He will take great delight in you.

—ZEPHANIAH 3:17 NIV

MONDAY

TUESDAY

WEDNESDAY

THURSDAY

FRIDAY

SATURDAY

SUNDAY

God is my salvation; I will trust and not be afraid. The LORD,
the LORD himself, is my strength and my defense. —ISAIAH 12:2 NIV

MONTH:

MONDAY

TUESDAY

WEDNESDAY

THURSDAY

FRIDAY

SATURDAY

SUNDAY

When the Lord saw her, his heart overflowed with compassion. "Don't cry!" he said. —LUKE 7:13 NLT

MONDAY

TUESDAY

WEDNESDAY

THURSDAY

FRIDAY

SATURDAY

SUNDAY

Since we have been made right in God's sight by faith, we have peace with God because of what Jesus Christ our Lord has done for us. —ROMANS 5:1 NLT

MONTH:

MONDAY

TUESDAY

WEDNESDAY

THURSDAY

FRIDAY

SATURDAY

SUNDAY

Not to us, O Lord, not to us, but to your name give glory,
for the sake of your steadfast love and your faithfulness! —PSALM 115:1 ESV

Imitate God, therefore, in everything you do, because you are his dear children. Live a life filled with love, following the example of Christ. He loved us and offered himself as a sacrifice for us, a pleasing aroma to God.

—EPHESIANS 5:1–2 NLT

MONTH:

MONDAY

TUESDAY

WEDNESDAY

THURSDAY

FRIDAY

SATURDAY

SUNDAY

Give your burdens to the LORD, and he will take care of you. —PSALM 55:22 NLT

MONDAY

TUESDAY

WEDNESDAY

THURSDAY

FRIDAY

SATURDAY

SUNDAY

The love of God is a reality among us: God sent His only Son into the world
so that we could find *true* life through Him. —1 JOHN 4:9 VOICE

MONTH:

MONDAY

TUESDAY

WEDNESDAY

THURSDAY

FRIDAY

SATURDAY

SUNDAY

"I am the bread of life. Whoever comes to me will never go hungry,
and whoever believes in me will never be thirsty." —JOHN 6:35 NIV

MONDAY

TUESDAY

WEDNESDAY

THURSDAY

FRIDAY

SATURDAY

SUNDAY

We know that in all things God works for the good of those who love him. —ROMANS 8:28 NIV

MONDAY

TUESDAY

WEDNESDAY

THURSDAY

FRIDAY

SATURDAY

SUNDAY

The eyes of the LORD are toward the righteous, and His ears are toward their cry for help. —PSALM 34:15 NASB

MONDAY

TUESDAY

WEDNESDAY

THURSDAY

FRIDAY

SATURDAY

SUNDAY

God . . . will supply all your needs from his glorious riches, which have been given to us in Christ Jesus.

—PHILIPPIANS 4:19 NLT

MONTH:

MONDAY

TUESDAY

WEDNESDAY

THURSDAY

FRIDAY

SATURDAY

SUNDAY

Our LORD, no other gods compare with you—Majestic and holy!
Fearsome and glorious! Miracle worker! —EXODUS 15:11 CEV

MONTH:

MONDAY

TUESDAY

WEDNESDAY

THURSDAY

FRIDAY

SATURDAY

SUNDAY

The earth is the LORD'S, and everything in it, the world, and all who live in it. —PSALM 24:1 NIV

MONTH:

MONDAY

TUESDAY

WEDNESDAY

THURSDAY

FRIDAY

SATURDAY

SUNDAY

Since we are living by the Spirit, let us follow the Spirit's leading in every part of our lives.

—GALATIANS 5:25 NLT

MONTH:

MONDAY

TUESDAY

WEDNESDAY

THURSDAY

FRIDAY

SATURDAY

SUNDAY

Let your conversation be always full of grace, seasoned with salt. —COLOSSIANS 4:6 NIV

MONDAY

TUESDAY

WEDNESDAY

THURSDAY

FRIDAY

SATURDAY

SUNDAY

MONDAY

TUESDAY

WEDNESDAY

THURSDAY

FRIDAY

SATURDAY

SUNDAY

Do nothing out of selfish ambition or vain conceit. Rather, in humility
value others above yourselves. —PHILIPPIANS 2:3 NIV

MONTH:

MONDAY

TUESDAY

WEDNESDAY

THURSDAY

FRIDAY

SATURDAY

SUNDAY

Put into action the generosity that comes from your faith. —PHILEMON 1:6 NLT

MONTH:

MONDAY

TUESDAY

WEDNESDAY

THURSDAY

FRIDAY

SATURDAY

SUNDAY

The path we walk is charted by faith, not by what we see with our eyes. —2 CORINTHIANS 5:7 VOICE

MONTH:

MONDAY

TUESDAY

WEDNESDAY

THURSDAY

FRIDAY

SATURDAY

SUNDAY

For we are his workmanship, created in Christ Jesus for good works,
which God prepared ahead of time for us to do. —EPHESIANS 2:10 CSB

If anyone speaks,
they should do so as one
who speaks the very words
of God. If anyone serves, they
should do so with the strength
God provides, so that in all
things God may be praised
through Jesus Christ. To him
be the glory and the power
for ever and ever. Amen.

—1 PETER 4:11 NIV

MONTH:

MONDAY

TUESDAY

WEDNESDAY

THURSDAY

FRIDAY

SATURDAY

SUNDAY

And what does the LORD require of you? To act justly and to love mercy
and to walk humbly with your God. —MICAH 6:8 NIV

MONTH:

MONDAY

TUESDAY

WEDNESDAY

THURSDAY

FRIDAY

SATURDAY

SUNDAY

He is so rich in kindness and grace that he purchased our freedom
with the blood of his Son and forgave our sins. —EPHESIANS 1:7 NLT

MONTH:

MONDAY

TUESDAY

WEDNESDAY

THURSDAY

FRIDAY

SATURDAY

SUNDAY

"See, I have written your name on the palms of my hands." —ISAIAH 49:16 NLT

MONDAY

TUESDAY

WEDNESDAY

THURSDAY

FRIDAY

SATURDAY

SUNDAY

Let the whole earth shout to the LORD; be jubilant, shout for joy, and sing. —PSALM 98:4 CSB

MONTH:

MONDAY

TUESDAY

WEDNESDAY

THURSDAY

FRIDAY

SATURDAY

SUNDAY

God plays no favorites. —ACTS 10:34 VOICE

MONDAY

TUESDAY

WEDNESDAY

THURSDAY

FRIDAY

SATURDAY

SUNDAY

Every good and perfect gift is from above, coming down from the Father
of the heavenly lights, who does not change like shifting shadows. —JAMES 1:17 NIV

Bible Permissions

GOD HEARS HER

From Our Daily Bread Ministries, this planner is part of the God Hears Her collection, designed to bring inspiration and encouragement to women every day. Each product speaks to a woman's heart, lifts her up, and reminds her that God is bigger than the trials she faces. Go to godhearsher.org to find the God Hears Her podcast, blog, and other related products.

GOD HEARS HER

Seek and she will find